ELEMENTARY PIANO SOLOS
Schirmer's HALLOWEEN FAVORITES

Ed. 3828

ISBN 978-0-7935-0992-8

G. SCHIRMER, Inc.

DISTRIBUTED BY

HAL•LEONARD®
CORPORATION

7777 W. BLUEMOUND RD. P.O. BOX 13819 MILWAUKEE, WI 53213

T0050948

Schirmer's HALLOWEEN FAVORITES

We climbed the creaky stairs, swept away the lingering cobwebs, and slowly pushed open the squeaky door to the Schirmer attic. Once inside the dusty room full of old music, we began our search for some of the spookiest music ever written. And we found it!

Now a new generation of piano students can enjoy some of the same Halloween piano pieces their Moms and Dads played when they were young. Students will create an entire "Mystery Story" of "Halloween Highjinks" when the "Spooks!," "The Four O'Clock Ghost," and "The Attic Ghost" join other "Ghosts!" in a "Ghost Dance."

Written by some of the best composers of children's music – Louise Garrow, David Carr Glover, Mark Nevin, Maxwell Eckstein, and others – these proven HALLOWEEN FAVORITES capture the spirit of this ghostly holiday for all time.

GHOSTS!

Louise Garrow

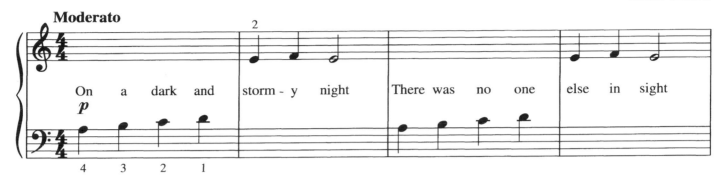

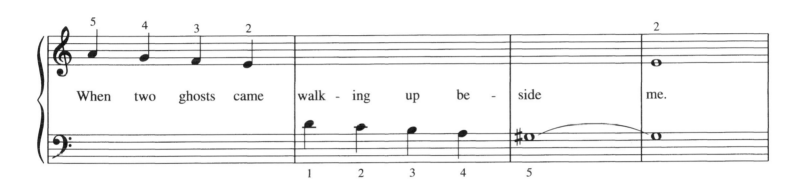

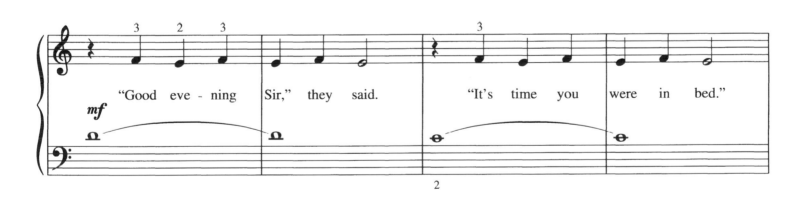

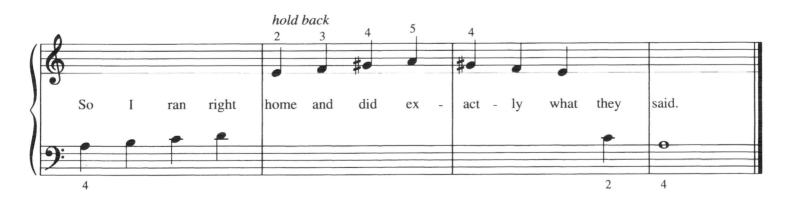

ATTIC GHOST

Samuel Wilson

Slowly, in a spooky manner

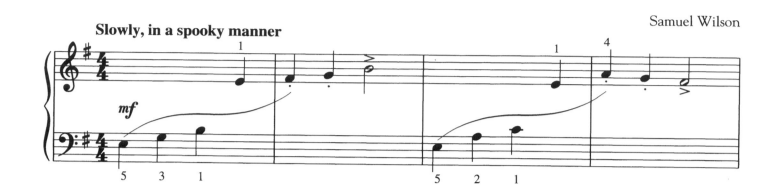

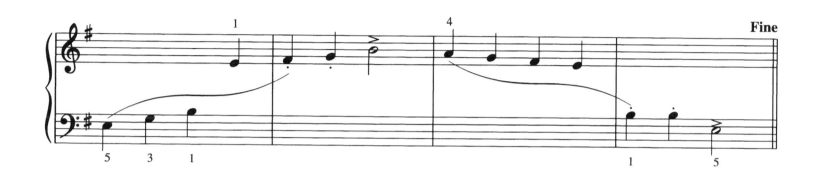

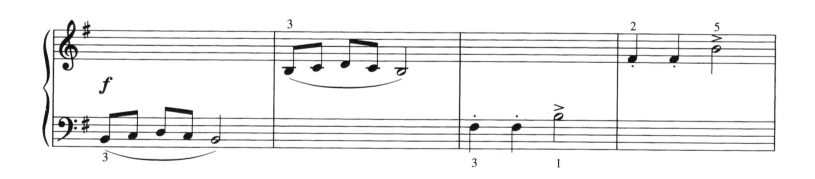

Blank for page turn

HALLOWEEN HIGH JINKS

Howard Kasschau

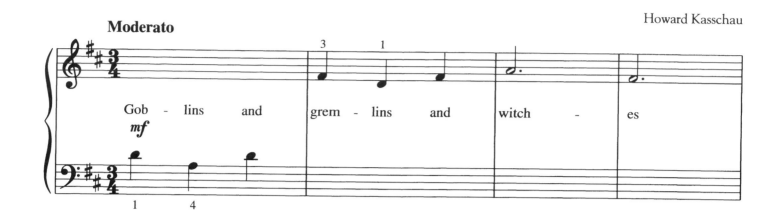

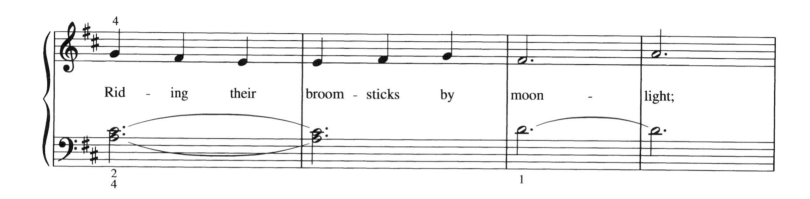

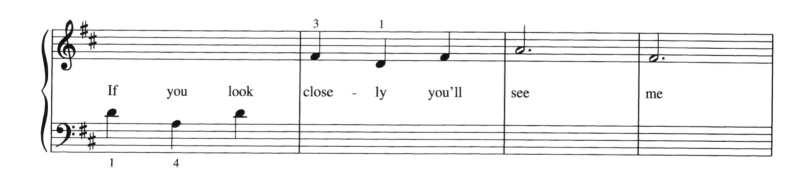

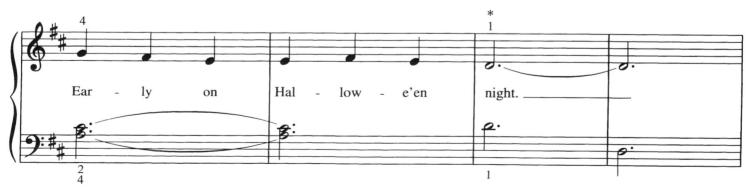

* Both thumbs on D.

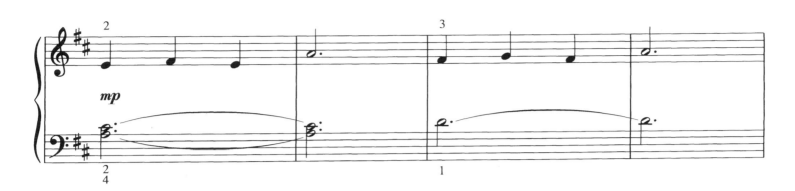

Low D

THE FOUR O'CLOCK GHOST

David Carr Glover

The clock strikes four (slowly)

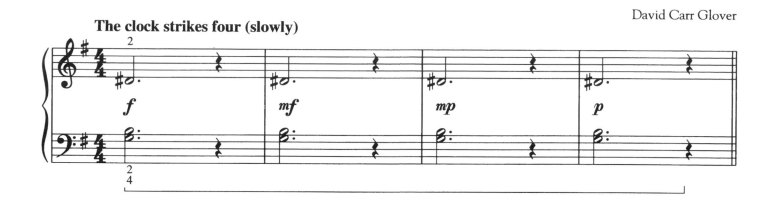

Moderately (never fast)

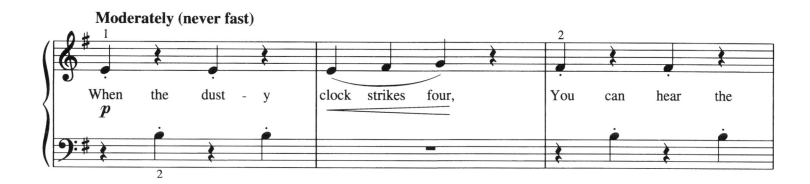

When the dust-y clock strikes four, You can hear the

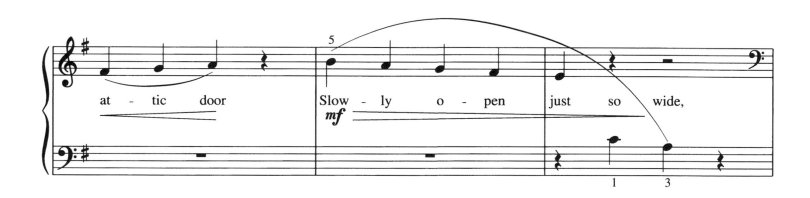

at-tic door   Slow-ly o-pen just so wide,

rit.   **A tempo**

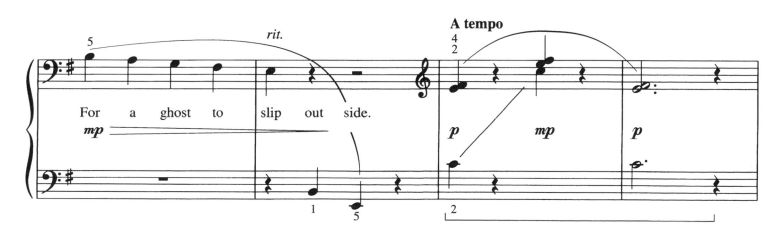

For a ghost to slip out side.

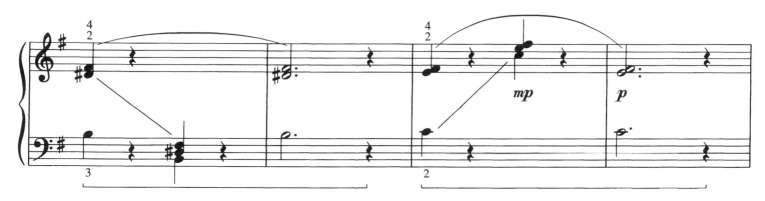

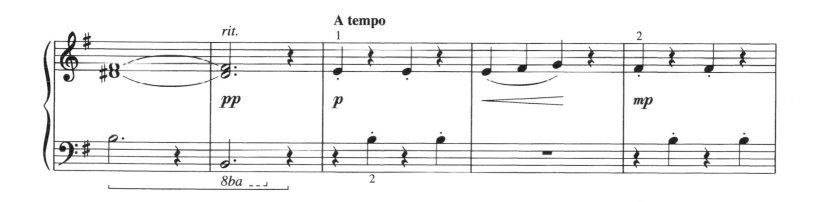

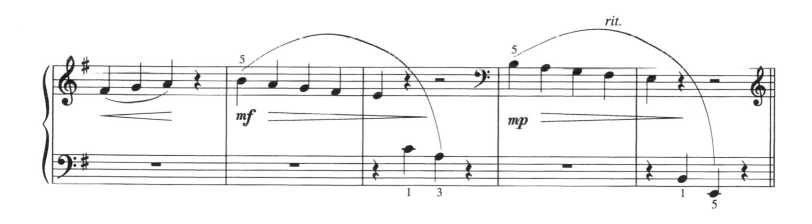

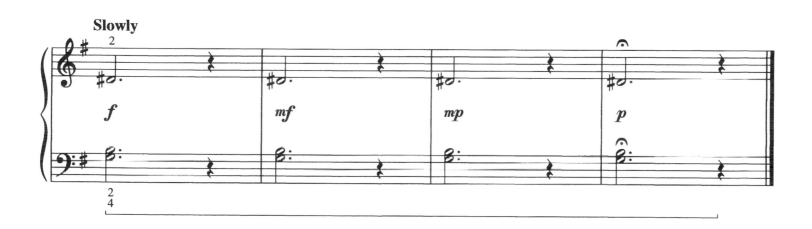

MYSTERY STORY

Mark Nevin

HALLOWEEN NIGHT

Mark Nevin

GHOST DANCE

T. Robin Maclachlan

Misterioso

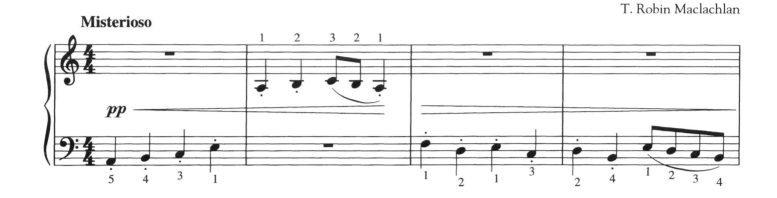

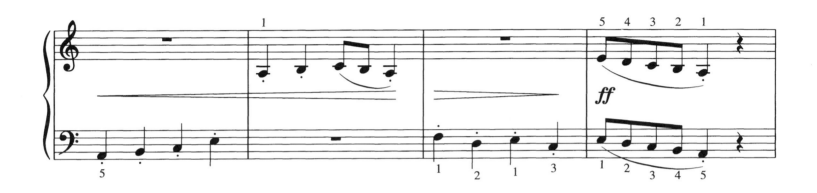

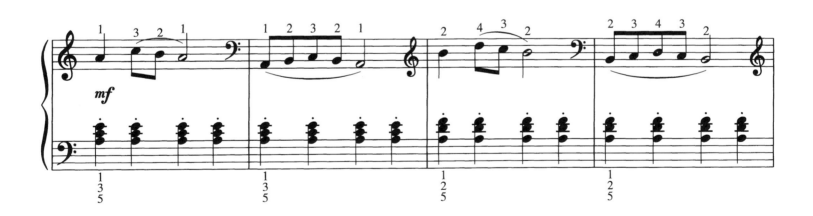

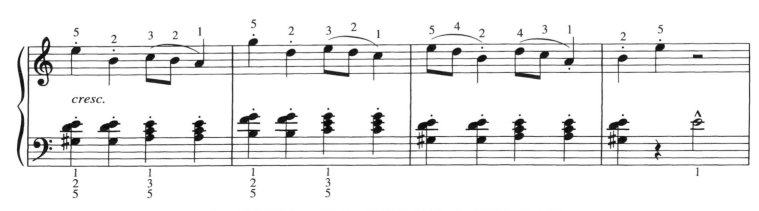

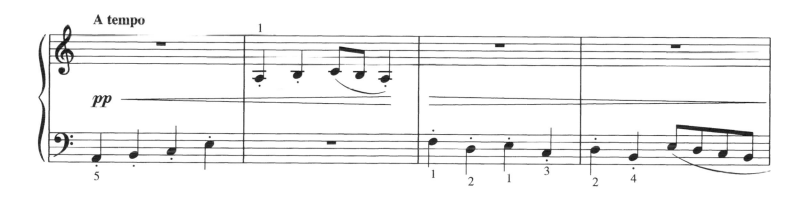

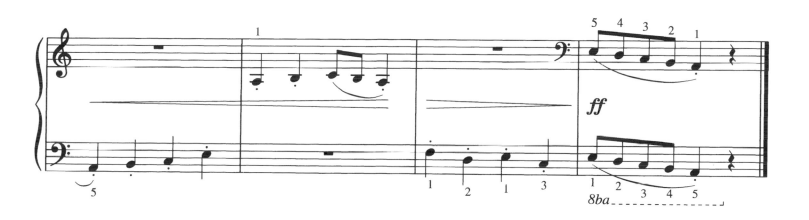

SPOOKS

You will hear ghost stories
Thrilling you through,
And then witches and spooks
Will be spoken of too;
But don't be afraid
It's all done for fun,
For twilight's the time
When these tales are spun.

Maxwell Eckstein

Mysteriously